INTERVIEW POWERFULLY AND GET HIRED

HOW TO GET HIRED ON YOUR TERMS

LISA RANGEL

COPYRIGHT © 2023 Chameleon Resumes LLC

This document is intended for private, individual use only by the individual purchasing the document. Transmission, distribution, duplication or public use by any means (electronic, mechanical, recording, photocopying or otherwise) is prohibited without express written consent from Chameleon Resumes.

ISBNs:

Paperback: 978-1-7333176-5-8

Ebook: 978-1-7333176-6-5

DISCLAIMER: While the author has used her best efforts in preparing and producing this ebook, she makes no guarantees, representations or warranties with the respect to the accuracy or completeness of the contents of this book and specifically disclaim any implied warranties for sale for fitness for a particular purpose. No warranty may be created or extended through affiliate or marketing partnerships in print or online sales and marketing materials. The advice and strategies contained herein are the opinions and based off client experiences of the author and may not be suitable for your situation. You should consult with a proper professional where appropriate. The author shall not be liable for any loss of profit, income or commercial damages, including but not limited to special, incidental, consequential or any other damage.

CONTENTS

Believe You Can Land a Job on Your Terms — v

1. Define Your Terms — 1
2. Rejection: What it is and what it isn't — 7
3. Preparing for Interviews: Set Yourself Apart from the Competition — 13
4. What to Wear to Impress on Your Interview — 35
5. Face the Difficult Questions Fearlessly — 41
6. How to Nail Phone Interviews — 51
7. Successful Video Interviewing Tips — 55
8. Be Armed for the "Do you have any questions for us?" Question — 61
9. Handling the Salary Question — 65
10. After the Interview — 71
    Conclusion — 75
    Next Steps — 77

    About the Author — 79
    Also by Lisa Rangel — 81

BELIEVE YOU CAN LAND A JOB ON YOUR TERMS

Landing a job on your terms is not out of your reach. Simply put: if you believe you can do it, you can do it! This is the essential starting point for your job search.

You may not know how you will get there or what specific steps to perform right now, but you must believe that, with the help of this book and other available resources, you can land a job that will complement your needs, desires, and life choices.

I can tell you that without this basic belief, landing a job on your terms will be very difficult to accomplish. However, if you're willing to believe you can do it and that the powers of the universe will work with you in your quest, then you have successfully accomplished the crucial first step to landing a job on your terms.

Of course, you already have this belief to some degree, or you wouldn't have invested in this book. So congratulations! You're already making progress toward your goal!

CHAPTER 1
DEFINE YOUR TERMS

Do you know what kind of job you want? This may seem like an obvious question, but many people start a job search without understanding what they want and what they don't want. They may have a vague idea—but a vague idea isn't enough to help you find a job you'll be happy in.

The next step to landing a job on your terms is to know exactly what your terms are. It is crucial to understand what you value in a job and an employer, and it's just as important to have a clear perspective on what you do not want in a job.

Without clarity on their terms, job seekers accept positions only to discover too late that they're unhappy with the duties, compensation packages, or corporate culture that accompany the new position.

Both parts of the equation—defining what you want and defining what you don't want—are equally essential to landing a job on your terms and avoiding emotional and professional turmoil in the process.

DEFINE WHAT YOU WANT

Make a list of what you want from your next position. What you desire will usually emerge if you look at a few areas that directly affect your life.

A few points to consider are:

Financial Requirements: You may know that you want to make a certain amount of money. You also know your desired compensation is within the realm of the skills, abilities, and experience you possess. Maybe you've not received a raise in three years and you realize you won't receive one at your current employer for reasons beyond your control. You might then put on your list that you want a 10% raise because you've done research that shows you have the skills and expertise to warrant this compensation bump.

Career Path: You may need to develop certain skills and connections in order to attain your long-term professional goals. Let's say that currently you are an oncology drug sales representative and your long-term goal is to manage a sales team within a firm that sells oncology drugs. You might decide to seek sales management jobs for products that support other diseases in order to gain management experience, then come back to oncology once you have this expertise. Sales management opportunities would then be an important item to add to your list.

Lifestyle Needs: You may need to land a role that supports your personal life. For example, you may need to work nights, or be home by 3 pm, or work from home 2-3 days per week. You may want a job that provides a company car you can also use for personal needs. It may be important to you to find a company that offers health insurance or tuition reimbursement. These points would go on your list.

Work Style Preferences: Do you like to work in team

environments? Do you prefer to work on your own? Do you like companies that value in-person meetings at the office or do you not want to travel to an office? Think long and hard about the situations that have suited you in the past and those where you were frustrated—and determine which options, if any, should be on your list.

Corporate Culture: Do you want an employer that values those who put their jobs first? Or do you want a role at a company where work/life balance is valued by all who work there? Do you want a job that will push you to make strides quickly in your career? Or do you want a job that will take second place to your full personal life? Personally, I have been in both situations and I can see the pros and cons of each, but what's important is that you know what matters to you.

Here are a few additional requirements you may have:

- Flexitime scheduling: It may not matter to you how many hours you work over 40 hours, but you may need flexibility in coming and going to accommodate your family life.
- Minimum salary: You may decide you need a salary not below a certain amount for any new job to be worth making the move. Make sure, however, that your desired salary is based on market realities. The key is to do the research to determine whether your skills, abilities and experiences warrant the salary you desire; otherwise, you may be wasting your time.
- Company size: Your long-term goal may be to work in a major, world-class corporation. If you're currently at a Fortune 1000 company, you may need to move to a much larger company in

order to gain the cultural experience that will allow you to end up at a Fortune 500 company. Company size would then be an important point to add to your list.

OUTLINE WHAT YOU DON'T WANT

You may be thinking, "Why should I outline what I don't want? It's simply the opposite of what I want." Well, for some people, this may be true. I have found, however, that for most people what they want and what they do not want are two entirely different lists, with little inverse correspondence between them.

Here are some examples of how the two lists can diverge:

- You may not want to travel overnight for your job —but day trips outside the office are ok with you. So overnight travel will be on your "don't want" list but day trips, while ok with you, would probably never make your "want" list.
- You may not want to work in a cubicle but you don't care if you have your own office, work in a group table setting, or work remotely at home— as long as you are not stuck in a tiny cube!
- You may not want to work past 6 pm at night but it's fine if the company wants you in occasionally at 7 am. I am sure, however, that getting in at 7 am regularly would not be on your "want" list.

WHY ARE THESE LISTS IMPORTANT?

The lists of what you want and what you don't want will define your job search parameters, interview answers, and compensation package negotiations. Without these spelled out, you have no way to:

- Define yourself to a prospective employer. This allows the employer to determine if you're a good fit for their company.
- Leverage and negotiate a fair package for the role for which you are being considered.
- Make yourself a memorable candidate to the prospective employer. The more one-size-fits-all you appear, the less appealing you are to an employer. You must be distinctive to be memorable.
- Avoid taking a job that does not meet your financial, professional, personal and lifestyle needs.

Your lists will help you evaluate job opportunities and formulate answers for interviews. Without these parameters, it may be tempting to consider jobs that do not fit your needs. You may then find yourself in a position that makes you unhappy in the months and years to come.

And there's another reason why your list of wants and don't-wants are important, too...

CHAPTER 2
REJECTION: WHAT IT IS AND WHAT IT ISN'T

The bottom line is: do not turn all rejections you experience into a negative reflection of who you are and your skills and experience. Frankly, it often is not that and all you're doing is negatively affecting your mindset. Your list of "needs/wants" and "don't wants" will help you handle rejection and maintain a positive mindset while looking for a job on your terms.

Often, a job offer doesn't come because the candidate was not the right fit because the needs and wants of the company didn't match the needs and wants of the candidate.

Clients, friends and associates who are job-searching will frequently say to me, "Ugh, I didn't get that job I applied for." I ask them the following questions to help them stay rooted in facts and stay positive:

(1) Do you know for a fact that someone else has filled the job?

Do you see on LinkedIn the name of someone newly hired, with the title of the job you sought? That would be proof. Did an announcement or press release go out naming the new hire in the role for which you interviewed? That would also be proof. Without proof, they haven't filled the job yet. If that's the case, you haven't been rejected... yet.

2 Are you sure the job is closed?

Find out if the job is still open. Especially in a challenging economy, companies may freeze their hiring budget. If the job is closed and they didn't hire anyone, then no-one was rejected for the role.

3 Are they still interviewing for the job?

Has the company ceased interviewing without making a hire? They may have put the position on hold. If they're not considering anyone for the role at this point and no decision is going to be made, no-one has been rejected.

4 When you interviewed, did you find you didn't want the job?

If you discovered you wouldn't want the job, and they then didn't offer you the job, were you really rejected? Does it matter that they didn't select you for a job you wouldn't have wanted?

5 When you interviewed, did you feel concerns about the position or the company?

Were you put off by anything the interviewer said? Did the company or job seem too unstructured or structured for you? Did the employer cite concerns about your educational or professional credentials? Were they seeking someone with a specific degree you don't possess? Did the employer say they wanted someone with expertise handling specific situations that you haven't encountered before?

If you had concerns about the job or the company, or if you felt the employer had concerns about your candidacy, you just may not be a good fit for that role. If you weren't a good fit, were you really rejected?

SO WHAT IS REJECTION?

After considering what rejection is not, I should tell you what I think rejection is, right? With job searching, rejection is:

If you wanted the job, were perfectly qualified according to the firm's requirements, and still did not get the job, then you were rejected.

While it is painful, there is nothing wrong with rejection. Getting rejected is part of life's natural selection process and is an inevitable by-product of making any sort of effort. You will be rejected from jobs. But why carry more rejection baggage than you need to?

If you didn't want the job, you were not rejected. If the job is still open, you were technically not rejected. If you had concerns about your background, education, or qualifications not measuring up to what they wanted, then you may not have fit the job's parameters. We sometimes label avoiding a poor fit as rejection, which can affect our ability to continue the job search with a positive spirit.

I suggest you view the job search as a quest for the right fit, rather than as a test of whether you are acceptable. This is where your list of needs/wants and don't wants can be especially helpful.

Example:

With the list of your needs/wants and don't wants, you can redefine what "getting rejected for a job" really means. Let's look at how this helps you.

Here are the sample lists of a job seeker named Jonathan. These are his wants:

- Wants to land a job as a marketing manager for a start-up firm focused on healthcare drug development that capitalizes on his oncology background.
- Needs to work remotely from home.
- Wants to work with an international team, specifically Asia and/or Europe.
- Needs a minimum salary of $95,000 plus incentives.

And his don't wants:

- Does not want to travel more than 15% of the year.
- Does not want to work in pediatric disease drug development.
- Does not want to use a corporate issued smart phone—wants to use his own.

Now we have a list of wants and don't wants, let's assume Jonathan lands interviews with four start-up drug firms over the course of two weeks. He does not advance in any of the roles. Here are the reasons he didn't land the job, for each company:

REJECTION: WHAT IT IS AND WHAT IT ISN'T

1. Syntegic Therapeutics: Requires travel 2 weeks per month.
2. Compass Technologies: Wants expertise in immunology, which he doesn't have.
3. Etanics, Inc.: Has a conservative, big-brother type technology policy.
4. Dyson Biotechnology Advisors: Base salary caps out at $135,000.

When you compare Jonathan's lists to the reasons he did not advance in the interview process at these companies, do you think he was rejected? I don't think so. He was simply not the right fit for the company and/or the company was not the right fit for him.

This exercise can help you develop and maintain a positive mindset as you look for the right job. Unnecessarily labeling your experiences as "rejection" can take its toll when you're applying to multiple positions and preparing for interviews. Do not apply the rejection label lightly. Use it only when it's applicable. And when it truly applies, use the experience to learn how you can improve your candidacy and perform better next time around.

CHAPTER 3

PREPARING FOR INTERVIEWS: SET YOURSELF APART FROM THE COMPETITION

The purpose of a company interview is twofold:

1. To learn whether you are a good cultural and performance fit for the company.
2. To see your response when handling stress—because an interview is a stressful situation.

An interview is meant to showcase your knowledge and your ability to think on your feet. The company is also evaluating how you present yourself in important situations. The interviewer assumes that the way you conduct yourself in the interview will be the way you conduct yourself with company executives, staff, vendors, and clients. So if you do something that seems questionable in the interview, they will assume you're at risk of doing something similar with other people.

Additionally, an interview can help you ascertain if this is a company you would like to join. Through discussion and questions, you can determine if this opportunity is a match for your skill set, professional goals, and lifestyle choices. Do not think the company holds all the cards. However, to ensure you get the chance to choose, you must play the interview game through to the end, which means you must start by thoroughly preparing for the meeting.

In today's economic climate, simply Googling the company before an interview will not set you apart from other candidates, and checking out the company's webpage no longer cuts it. In fact, a savvy interviewer can now tell if that's all you did. This type of minimal effort will reflect poorly on your candidacy and put you towards the bottom of the list.

Defining your needs/wants and don't wants in the manner discussed earlier and preparing for the interview as outlined below will best position you to move successfully through the interview process. You will then be equipped to make accurate decisions and secure a job on your terms.

HOW MUCH TIME DO YOU NEED TO PREPARE?

I am often asked how much time to allocate to interview preparation. There is no precise, formulaic answer. I wish I could say, "Prepare for X amount of time and you will be assured of landing the role." But there are some suggested time-frames to consider:

- Set aside a minimum of 3-5 hours to research the company, the position for which you are interviewing, and the interviewer(s).
- Allocate 5-10 hours to researching yourself and your preferences, and to practicing your answers to a full range of possible interview questions.

This will prepare you to think effectively on your feet in an interview.

It is at this point I might see raised eyebrows. You probably understand and accept the need to research the company, the position, and the interviewer. But when I suggest spending 5-10 hours educating yourself on, well, yourself, this is when I get the perplexed looks.

"I already know my background and myself, so why do I need to study myself?" may be the question in your mind. But the secret to successfully landing a job on your terms generally lies in the work you devote to answering this question.

WHY YOU NEED TO STUDY YOURSELF

I performed an informal poll of 50 clients and students, asking them the following questions regarding a recent interview they had:

(1) What percentage of time was spent discussing your background?

Most answered that 75% or more time was spent discussing their background.

(2) What percentage of time was spent discussing the company's products, history or performance?

Most answered that less than 30% of the time was spent discussing the firm's products, history or performance.

Note: This was not a scientific poll, nor were these

numbers supposed to add up to 100% even if it was a precise survey.

Candidates generally approach an interview thinking they need to prove to the prospective employer that they have exhaustively researched the firm and know everything there is to know about it. Yet most interviewers and hiring managers will not spend much time asking candidates to demonstrate this knowledge.

Hiring managers and interviewers already know their company. Yes, they may want to test how interested you are in the company and they may want to see whether you can apply your expertise to their organization. But generally speaking, most interviewers will spend time asking questions about you, your background, your preferences, your experiences, your achievements, your challenges, your failures, and how you can bring value to their corporation. Therefore:

Spend most of your prep time reviewing your background and practicing answers that show how you can make a positive difference to the company if hired.

RESEARCHING YOU

We prepare in this way in order to minimize the risk of having to think about something for the very first time during the interview. The goal is to have thought of most possible questions and practiced the best possible answers before the interview. You cannot predict every possible question, of course, but if you're prepared with clear and confident answers, you will think more effectively on your feet and your self-assurance will radiate though the interview.

Know your resume backwards, forwards and every angle in between:

- **Be intimately familiar with each and every bullet on your resume.** For each bullet on your resume, write out the story or a few examples outlining how you performed or achieved that particular bullet. Be able to succinctly and articulately communicate the story behind each bullet.
- **Readily know the numbers associated with each bullet and the information behind the numbers.** To leave the most favorable impression with your interviewer, take the numbers listed one step further and know how they came about. For example, if you know that you increased sales by 23%, know what the starting and ending revenue numbers were, which markets contributed to the increase and what changes you made to get the increase.
- **Prepare stories about challenges, failures, and difficult situations that are not on your resume.** These types of questions always come up. Embrace this fact and be ready for those questions. We will address specifics related to these in the "Face the Most Difficult Questions Fearlessly" section.

Prepare answers to the standard interview questions and be able to instantly recall these answers:

- **Tell me about yourself.** This is by far the most mundane question and it often reveals that your interviewer is either inexperienced or unimaginative. Nonetheless, you must be ready for this question with a concise, all-inclusive answer. Please do not start with your early years—the hiring manager is not asking for your biography. However, this is an opportunity to validate why they decided to see you. Offer a brief professional synopsis of your professional history and proudest achievements, along with a quick anecdote that adds something appropriately personal.

- **Why did you leave your last job?** If the reason you left is neutral or positive, express it confidently without revealing personal information—keep it professionally focused. If the reason is somewhat to downright negative, be prepared to present it in a neutral, but truthful light. The prospective employer does not need to know all the sordid details. A brief, diplomatic, and neutral answer is the best way to move the conversation along, so the hiring manager does not feel the need to delve further.
- **Why do you want to leave your current job?** If you are currently working, be sure that your reasons for wanting to leave are rooted in advancing your career and professional development. You should clearly explain how the prospective company will benefit from you pursuing these goals. The reasons should not be based on personality conflicts, comfort or convenience issues, compensation or benefits.
- **Describe your ideal boss or work arrangement.** Be sure to describe a manager profile or a work arrangement that exists at the company—

especially if the company is one where you want to work. On the other hand, do not simply say what they want to hear—or you may get hired and realize you don't like working for their type of boss or work culture. However, if you do want the job and you are flexible, be sure to describe a person or place that exists within that organization. Set the company up to succeed in making you happy if they hire you.

- **In explaining why you are pursuing a role you have done before, don't put your prospective manager's job down when describing why you're not pursuing the higher level job.** If they ask why you do not want to manage any longer, be sure that you don't denigrate the job your prospective manager has—or inadvertently appear to be looking down on your potential manager. No one really wants to hire someone who has that been-there-done-that feel and makes the manager feel dumb or inadequate. Be sure to answer from a point of wanting to contribute at a different level, and talk about how you want to make someone else look good as you know how it feels to be supported by a great team in your previous roles.
- **When answering questions posed by the interviewer, don't pontificate about how you used to do things.** Do not reference past incidents in a reminiscing or nostalgic capacity. When answering an interview question, describe a past experience objectively and diplomatically. Do not reminisce or pontificate. No one wants to hire a blowhard or a know-it-all. Always come

across curious to new approaches or situations and do not make it seem like all your previous solutions will solve all future problems. You will come across like you could be blindsided by thinking you know and have done everything.

- **Ask about what issues are motivating the company to make the hire.** Then outline how you can solve the current issues. Inquire about what challenges the company is currently experiencing and ask diagnostic questions humbly and inquisitively, where appropriate. You want to demonstrate how you would approach a problem, without making the employer feel stupid that they didn't think of what you might ask… you want your questions to come across like you're trying to be helpful and supportive.
- **What are your strengths? What personality traits have contributed to your success?** This is an opportunity to sell yourself and provide concrete, specific examples of work experiences that demonstrate your strengths. Stick to strengths that complement the position for which you're applying. Ensure they're relevant to the organization, the job and the company's goals.
- **What areas do you need to further develop or need training on?** This is the "What are your weaknesses?" question in positive guise. Answer the question in a similar, positive but sincere manner: "I would benefit from public speaking training" or "I could benefit from time management classes so I don't take on too many projects." Answer this question as you would any

question about your deficiencies: (1) Remember that everyone has weaknesses, so don't refuse to acknowledge yours. (2) Do not bring up a weakness that could suggest you would not perform well at the job. (3) Demonstrate how you have improved your skill set or compensated for your weakness to ensure it is never an issue at the job.

- **What do you like to do outside of work?** Be genuine in this answer. It is a chance for the hiring manager to see you as a person and not as just another applicant. The smart way to approach this question is to choose a hobby that can define you as interesting, driven, self-motivated, or unique. It should add dimension to you as a person. Do not bring up any activity that is controversial, based in politics or religion, displays poor judgment, depicts you as lazy, or could interfere with your job performance or attendance.

- **Tell me about a typical day/week/month in your job at X company. What did you like most/least about your last role?** Be colorful and specific when describing what you do in a day/week/month at your job. Assume the interviewer has no idea what you do. Even if they know what a marketing manager does at their company, they have no idea what that entails at your company. So do not assume they know—they don't. Offering a descriptive picture of your work activities, interactions and results demonstrates to the hiring manager that you have a great understanding of your role and take pride in your position. People who provide vague or general answers either did not do the job as stated, are not proud of what they did, or are poor communicators of what they did—none of which is attractive to an employer. As a side note, the worst possible answer, in my opinion, is, "I did everything." Do not ever say that. It tells the hiring manager nothing more than that you are full of yourself. Offer specifics if you want to make a positive impact.

- **Tell me about a problem you had with a client/boss/employee and how you handled it.** Companies want to hire inventive, resilient employees who can troubleshoot unexpected situations effectively with little or no drama in the workplace. Employers do not expect prospective employees to have never had a problem—everyone runs into difficulties at work. But you set yourself apart from other applicants when you demonstrate your skill in handling these problems and your ability to learn from them. Describe a time you and your boss disagreed on a project and how you handled yourself. Outline a customer complaint that arose, how you identified the problem, and how you fixed it. Diplomatically describe working with a confrontational employee and how you resolved the situation or even turned it around. Describe your experience in a neutral, humble, and solution-driven manner. Your answers and your demeanor will tell the interviewer how you will perform when problems arise in their company.

- **Why do you want to work for us?** To effectively answer this question, you have to have researched yourself and the interviewing company. Once you have this research under your belt, you can provide an answer that demonstrates how your experience and abilities make an excellent match with the company and the position it is seeking to fill. You want to show the compatibility between your aspirations and the company's objectives. Simply put, if you hit your goals, the company will hit their goals. Companies want to hire employees whose personal goals are aligned with the goals of the organization.
- **Why should we hire you?** This is your time to shine. Based on the research you've done and the information you've gleaned from the interview, outline succinctly how your experience and skills will allow you to fully satisfy the company's needs. Describe how you will bring value by helping them exceed their goals. The answer you give should put to rest in the interviewer's mind, "Is this the right candidate? The best candidate? How do I know?" If you answer those questions for the interviewer, you will be advanced to the next level, or if this is the final interview, you will be offered the job.

RESEARCHING THE COMPANY, THE INTERVIEWER, AND THE POSITION

Researching the company is a must, and almost all job candidates do it to some degree today. However, many candidates do not do the work thoroughly or methodically—which presents an opportunity for the motivated job seeker. I will address here some of the basic steps, to ensure your efforts are thorough, but I also provide many less obvious research tools to ensure you stand out from other applicants.

The emphasis in all my tips is that you shouldn't simply study the information outlined in corporate, public, and third-party sources. Anyone can do that. The interview is not a test to see whether you read the company website. Instead, you want to identify opportunities and demonstrate how you can add value to the company, if they hire you. Take the information you gain through your research and prepare insightful questions and observations that can serve as discussion points during the interview. Here are some ways to do that:

Check the company website for information—and not just in the usual places.

Don't just check out the company history and mission statement—look at every page on the website and try to deduce where the company is headed and how you can contribute to their mission.

- Review the company's products and services and get a handle on how they present themselves to the marketplace. What image do they put forth?
- Get a sense of the management's career histories and see what professional and educational credentials are valued by the firm. Are executives home grown and have been with the company for a while? Do they tend to get recruited from competitors? Are their backgrounds a little unorthodox for the position they hold?

- Look at all the job openings. What kinds of positions are being filled? Does this tell you anything about the company or give you information about its direction? For example, you may notice that the company seems to be expanding its sales force. If you're interviewing for a training role, you could then indicate you have observed that many sales people may be hired and ask how the company expects the training team to contribute to their on-boarding.

Google the company's name for articles written by third parties.

Look for third-party commentary and see how it supplements, supports or contradicts the information written by the company. This outside information can offer additional insights. How is the third-party information different or similar to the company's take on the same subjects?

- Research stories about the company on Forbes.com, Fortune.com, huffingtonpost.com, major news outlets and industry publications. Do they contain comments made by the company's spokespeople? This will give you a sense of the interviewer's opinions on these stories.
- The Better Business Bureau can be a helpful source of information for smaller companies with whom you may be interviewing.
- Google the company's name and the words <complaints>, <problems>, <unhappy employees> or <scam> if you have any concerns

about the company. This will reveal whether any adverse information has been documented or written about the firm.

Look up the firm on glassdoor.com or thevault.com to find out what is said about the firm by its employees.

- Examine the stats provided by these sites and read what employees say about the firm. If you find negative points, are these things you can live with—or better yet, would you thrive within that type of environment? One person's "boring job" may be another person's "stable employer."
- Remember to take the information in its context, as every firm has unhappy employees and these may be the ones who take the time to write negative commentary.

Review financial information if the company is public, on edgar-online.com or Yahoo Finance.

- This is a crucial action, regardless of the position to which you are applying. It is imperative that you understand the business and financial underpinnings of any potential employer.
- If you are a creative professional, do not think you're excused from understanding the financials of a company. You should understand how your creative contributions will affect the company's top and bottom lines. Knowing the business of your craft is one of the best ways you can differentiate yourself as a creative professional.

- If you are a financial or business professional, take the time to review the company's overall financial position. Showing that you have some understanding even of areas that you won't be directly responsible for is a key way to differentiate yourself as a solid business person.

Follow the company prior to the interview on all its relevant social media channels.

- What is the company talking about? What is it tweeting and posting? What are the obvious and underlying themes you observe? Can you apply any of your previous experiences to some of these topics being discussed in social media channels?
- Are they featuring promotions, sales, special events or product launches? How could you contribute to their success?
- Are they particularly proud of a charitable initiative in which they are involved? What can you offer this initiative? Be prepared to discuss it.

Consider speaking to past or current employees of the company, and more specifically, to people from the department to which you are applying.

- Be selective here. Use your judgment and consider the source behind the information when you have an opportunity to do this.
- You can use LinkedIn to find past and current employees and discover how you are connected

to them. You can then evaluate if an introduction would be helpful and prudent.

Have a strong handle on the firm's position in its marketplace and how it ranks in comparison to its competitors.

- It is not enough to simply know who the company's competitors are. Take it further by understanding how the company is viewed in the marketplace and how its customers rate it.
- If this information is not available publicly, do your own research. Speak to contacts in the industry, gather their impressions and observations, and ask for suggestions.

RESEARCHING THE INTERVIEWER

When interviewing, one of your goals is to create rapport with the interviewer and begin the cultivation of a relationship. Researching the interviewer can therefore give you insights to use during the course of your conversation. Keep in mind that some of this information may not be usable. But having the information is better than not having it: the insights can help you say the right thing and avoid committing a gaffe.

Research the person on LinkedIn and Google.

- Look for possible conversation points and common interests. File these in the back of your mind to use if the opportunity presents itself.
- See if they have attended any professional conferences recently, as that could make for an

interesting discussion about industry trends and best practices.
- Explore whether you have worked for the same or competitor organizations.
- Determine if you share the same alma mater. In most cases, this piece of information can be a good thing to reference. However, not everyone had a positive experience in college, as I was reminded when one of my clients mentioned to an interviewer that they'd gone to the same school. Apparently the interviewer did not share her enthusiasm for the school, and this cast a dark cloud over the remainder of the interview.

Become familiar with the person's career path.

- This can be good information for interviews with the management and staff people that you may work with, if hired.
- You can determine whether to ask them how they achieved their success or ask for their experiences with certain initiatives.

Use information from Facebook and other personal websites with caution.

- If you find that your interviewer has a public Facebook account and has (knowingly or unknowingly) told the world that she breeds Great Danes or that he recently took his four children to Vermont, think twice before bringing up this information. You may wish to demonstrate your superb research skills but the

interviewer may come away thinking you are a creepy stalker who is trying to bond superficially.
- Dropping information found from social media channels can be the equivalent of name-dropping to prove what and who you know. It can make you look immature and unsophisticated and may not advance your candidacy forward.
- If the interviewer mentions that he recently went to Vermont, by all means ask him about the trip. Or if asked about your hobbies, you may bring up your passion for competing in the Westminster Dog Show with your prize chocolate labrador. But use judgment when demonstrating what you have discovered about the person who is interviewing you.

RESEARCHING THE POSITION

Thoroughly understanding the position for which you are applying is absolutely essential. With this information you can start to outline point by point how your experiences and credentials will enable you to successfully perform the role. How do you learn all you can about the open role?

Ask the corporate human resources contact or the search firm recruiter for the job description.

You want to do this for two reasons:

1. The job description is different than the job ad posting. The job ad posting is written to attract candidates to apply to the company. The job description defines the expectations, credentials, and requirements needed to be successful in the role.

2. As a former recruiter, I was always more impressed with candidates who asked for a job description, versus those who did not ask. It showed me who was going the extra mile. Knowing the job description allows you to explain how you can perform each aspect of the role, with examples drawn from your past experience. So give yourself the advantage and ask for it. If the corporate HR contact or the search firm recruiter does not have it or cannot provide it, don't fret. It is still better to ask than not to ask.

Research the job title at competitor firms.

- Job titles may mean different things at different companies. A director of marketing in one company may oversee some aspect of sales, whereas in another firm, the director of marketing reports into the sales department, and in yet a third company, the director of marketing may be a peer to the director of sales.
- Get a sense of what is contained within the job's responsibilities and have a sense of how this role is structured at other firms. You will not bring up the other firms during your interview but the information can shed light on how the available position is structured and can help you make sure that you do want this job.

Prepare examples of how you have performed or would perform each aspect listed on the job description.

- Be ready to provide tactical examples of how you can successfully perform the duties and requirements listed.
- Write down these points as preparation for the interview. I suggest writing your examples on paper, rather than just thinking about them. This will help organize your thoughts. The first time you come up with your examples should NOT be during the actual interview. Write out and practice saying these points.

Use LinkedIn to find people who used to hold the position title for which you are interviewing.

- You are not looking to connect with these people and this will probably not be information you will share on the interview, but look at that person's background. What were their past positions? What is this person's education? Do you have a similar or different background?
- Do you have the impression that the new person being hired will be expected to fix a problem, grow a unit, or create something new? Does it seem to you that the person who previously held the position could not do this—or did it well?
- Is it a good thing your background is similar (the company wants someone with a similar experience set) or a bad thing (the company wants someone from a different industry or business angle)? In either case, you must demonstrate that your experience is appropriate and valuable.

Now you're prepared for the interview conversation, it's time to think about that first impression. What will you wear?

CHAPTER 4
WHAT TO WEAR TO IMPRESS ON YOUR INTERVIEW

I know that job seekers reading this book are pretty savvy, and you might think that we don't need to cover this topic, given all the information available on the subject. But with all the changes in corporate dress standards, the divergence of company cultures, and the rise of freelancing, it turns out that interview attire is something that can never be covered enough.

Here's the basic rule: what you are wearing during your job interview should never distract from your purpose, which is to convey that you are the right candidate for the open role. Standing out on an interview is important—but you do not want your clothes to do that for you. The key point to keep in mind:

Your clothes should not be louder than you.

If you wear the right outfit to an interview, people will most likely not notice what you wore. But if you wear the wrong thing to an interview, your outfit could be the only thing the interviewer remembers—which would be a disaster. If the discussion following your interview is about what you wore, as opposed to what you can do, you have missed your opportunity.

When deciding what to wear to an interview, remember that you always want to be the most formally dressed person in the room. This is true regardless of whether you're going into a conservative environment or a casual one. I am not referring to ballroom formal here—I'm talking about effort. Put another way: the interviewer should not look more pulled together than the job seeker. For instance, the interviewer should not be wearing khakis and a blue button-down shirt, while the interviewee is wearing jeans and a blue button-down shirt. The other way around, however, is acceptable.

Here are some tips to help you steer the right course.

FOR TRADITIONAL COMPANIES AND CORPORATE POSITIONS

- A blue or black suit is still very much the standard for both men and women. Pants suits for women are acceptable.
- Keep complementary items (shirts, blouses, ties) to neutrals such as white, cream, oxford blue, or navy blue.
- Shoes should be conservative and match the suit in most cases. For women, shoes should be heeled and closed-toed.

Jewelry and accessories:

- Watches should be professional looking, with a leather or metal band; no plastic bands.

- Earrings, bracelets and necklaces should be close to the body and conservative. Do not wear anything that is dangling or noisy.
- Perfume or cologne: I say avoid it. The interviewer may dislike your choice, or worse, have an allergy or sensitivity to the scent you are wearing.

FOR CREATIVE COMPANIES AND POSITIONS

When interviewing at a creative company or for a creative position (i.e. art director, head designer, designer, graphic artist), it can be challenging to demonstrate your design flair without bringing negative attention to yourself. You probably need to be stylish in your attire and presentation materials, but you risk making the wrong choices. If you're going for this type of interview, however, you have probably accepted this risk. In any case, you may not land the job if you don't take the risk of standing out.

Here are ways to optimize your chances of taking the right sartorial risk:

- Do your research and use your judgment. If you're interviewing at a progressive technology start-up and your recruiter says, "Don't wear a suit," then do not wear a suit. Khakis and a crisp, blue button-down shirt are acceptable.
- Even if your research reveals that everyone wears jeans and T-shirts to work, I would still not wear jeans and a T-shirt to the interview. Unless you are specifically told by a reputable employee contact, recruiter, or HR to wear jeans and a T-

shirt, you should still err on the side of conservative and wear khakis and a crisp, button-down shirt.
- If you are interviewing for a creative role in a fashion or accessories company, wearing items that demonstrate your creativity or use of their product line is smart. Abide by the rule that "your clothes should not be louder than you" and you will be just fine.
- For women, wearing skirts or dresses on interviews with more casual companies is acceptable, as long as the outfit is tastefully accessorized and confidently pulled together.

ACCESSORIES FOR ANY INTERVIEW

An interview is where you are supposed to put forth your best efforts. If your best includes questionable choices, the employer is left wondering what will happen once they hire you. Remember the choices you make for an interview reflect the quality of your judgment.

Here are general tips to keep in mind when preparing for your interview:

- Bring a leather (or similar looking material) portfolio with a pad of paper, pen, and section to keep business cards (your own and those you receive).
- Have 5 to 10 copies of your resume and a list of references with company, title, relationship, and contact information.
- Carry one bag—this holds true even for women. Carrying more than one bag can look sloppy. The

exception to this is if the candidate needs to carry a portfolio or laptop for the interview. But in these cases, make sure that all items look professional and presentable.
- Make sure everything fits properly: no ill-fitting clothing or accessories.
- Double-check clothing and accessories by sitting, standing, and walking around to ensure your outfit is comfortable and modest in all situations. You do not want to be tugging at your waist band, neckline, skirt hem, or shirt buttons. Give your outfit a test drive before the event.
- Have clothes cleaned and pressed professionally before each interview.
- Smile! Always go into the interview with a great outlook, a positive mindset, and a smile on your face. Employers want to hire people with good energy who will contribute positively to the company.
- Do not over-answer any question. Offer your answer in a conversational manner, but do not provide too much information: this suggests insecurity, nervousness, or a desire to please. Confidence comes from knowing when you said enough, and then stopping.

Dressing well isn't just about what other people see; if you know you look good, you'll derive confidence from that, enabling you to face your interview and any tricky questions fearlessly. Speaking of which—let's talk about those difficult questions.

CHAPTER 5
FACE THE DIFFICULT QUESTIONS FEARLESSLY

Over the past few years, many people have had to face job and income losses, lowered expectations and results, client losses, workforce reductions, office closings, and more. If you have experienced these difficulties, you are in good company.

Employed individuals going into job interviews today often have concerns about how to handle questions regarding disappointing personal or company track records over the past three or four years. Unemployed candidates must enter interviews carrying the psychological baggage that comes from being without a job. They wonder how to respond when asked why they haven't been hired, why they were released in the first place, whether they have maintained their skills, etc.

So the best way to approach a job search under these conditions is to remember:

Relatively few people can claim a linear, progressive, and positive career path over the past few years. In fact, I believe most people have experienced some minor to significant professional setback since 2008.

You will reduce your anxieties about job interviews if you accept these two ideas:

1. People hire people they like. Be personable and likable so the hiring manager feels like they can work with you each day. If the hiring manager likes you, it can overcome many perceived issues with a candidate's background. You will be surprised what a hiring manager will put aside if they connect well with the candidate and feel they can work with the person each and every day. Do not underestimate this.
2. Accept any setbacks you've experienced as a result of the economic downturn and be prepared to discuss them gracefully, honestly, and diplomatically. After all, you cannot avoid talking about your recent work history; if you do, hiring managers will think you're hiding something. And all other things being equal, I believe the candidate who can speak in a positive manner about their challenges wins the game. Your honesty and self-confidence will greatly increase your creditability with the hiring manager. It will also demonstrate how you would conduct yourself as an employee if hired.

If your recent past contains setbacks, do not try to hide them and simply hope the interviewer will not ask about them. It is far better to fully expect to be asked difficult questions and be prepared to provide answers that display your strength in adversity. And most importantly, be likable and confident throughout the process.

FACE THE DIFFICULT QUESTIONS FEARLESSLY

Here are general rules for handling any challenging points in your work history:

- Always focus on the silver lining of any negative situation and explain how you improved as a person because of the experience.
- Describe negative situations as "challenges" and never as "problems."
- Do not say anything negative about anyone. EVER! From a hiring manager's perspective, there are always two sides of a story and somewhere in the middle is the truth. Always be diplomatic. If you speak poorly about a previous boss or co-worker, you can easily be viewed as a future problem/complainer/troublemaker. No employer wants to hire this type of worker.
- When pressed about a negative situation, always weave in what you learned from the situation versus what the other person did wrong and how it affected you.

Here are specific, yet common, situations job seekers face, with guidance on how to handle them fearlessly:

FIRED?

If you have been fired, prepare a diplomatic way to convey this and focus on what you learned from the event. An example of how to answer why you left a firm could be something like:

"Management decided the position I held was not the best fit for me and I was released to find a role that was better suited for my skills. I enjoyed working with accounts and ensuring their needs and requests were serviced. This resulted in my producing significant new income from up-selling services. My boss and I thought I would be great at sales since I was already generating a solid income stream. So when a sales position became open, I jumped at the opportunity, even though it was a risk.

In hindsight, I was not as skilled at cultivating new contacts as I was at nurturing existing relationships, so I struggled with the new position. I attended training and performed countless hours of role-playing on my own time to improve my skills in this area, but I just could not improve to the levels needed to succeed in the role. My previous role was now filled and unavailable for me. So we agreed that I would leave my position amicably, as I have no regrets trying something new that challenged me. It also helped me to learn that I really enjoy working with clients on large-scale initiatives, which is why I'm looking to return to that type of role in a larger capacity."

HAD A DIFFICULT BOSS?

If you had a difficult boss in your work history, embrace that experience. Don't fight it. Accept that this person came into your life to teach you things about yourself that you did not know and would not have learned otherwise.

With that in mind, ask yourself: what did working for this difficult person teach me about myself? What made them difficult to work for? What part did I contribute to the conflict? What did I learn about my part and how did I correct my actions? By answering these questions, you can start to formulate an answer that will position your challenging situation as a growth opportunity.

Here is a sample answer that could be given in answering the common interview question, "Tell me about the most difficult person you worked for in your career."

> The most challenging person I worked for would probably be ___<insert name here> ___ at ___<Insert company name here> ___. He was difficult to work for because he worked around the clock with exceptionally high standards. While admittedly it was sometimes not pleasant to answer an email on a Saturday morning at 7 am (said with a smile), I understood the importance of responding quickly to our demanding clientele. I was always available to ensure our clients were satisfied. I appreciate the fact that ___<insert name here> ___ was demanding, as I was able to prove to him and to myself that I can produce quality work in tight time frames under extreme pressure. Before working for him, I did not know that I was capable of that and so I am grateful for that opportunity.

WORKED WITH A LESS THAN COOPERATIVE CO-WORKER?

The company may want to get a glimpse of how you would deal with colorful characters on their staff. If asked about how you have dealt in the past with challenging co-workers, do not focus on what the person did wrong to you. Describe what you learned from the situation and how you can handle a variety of challenging people.

Here is an example of how you can model the answer:

> "Generally speaking, personalities are going to vary within staffs and I fully accept that. While I aim to get along with

everyone, I realize that situations can arise where people may not like me or my work style. If this happens, and luckily it does not happen often, I aim to stick to the work issue at hand and not engage in any personal commentary that can be misconstrued. I ensure that deadlines, directions and deliverables are clear on both sides and get the project qualitatively off my plate as quickly as possible. I don't look to be right in confrontational situations. I try to advocate for items that are in the company's best interest."

If you are actually asked about a specific person and pinned to discuss it, be cautiously diplomatic. Do not necessarily think the best answer is giving the interviewer the dirt they seem to want to hear. It can be a trap to see if you fall for it and let your guard down. So, again, stick to what you learned versus gossiping about anyone else. Here is an example:

"Yes, working with accounting and business operations as a creative professional can be a challenge, since what is creatively demanded in the marketplace may not always be the most cost-effective solution. This was particularly true with the CFO of our company. He stuck strictly to the numbers and did not factor in any information that was not quantified or documented by research. I was frustrated at times but I did not fight it. As a result of his consistent position, I have become an expert on the business of my craft. While you might not want me as your CFO (said with a smile), I now give rational information backed up by research and examples to support any creative option that I'm advocating. My CFO's challenging position has made me a better creative leader."

EXPERIENCED MARKET SHARE LOSS, CLIENT DEPARTURES, OR SALES/PROFIT DECREASES IN THE PAST 3 TO 5 YEARS?

If you have experienced business losses, you probably do not want to brag about them but you should not avoid discussing them if asked. Any obvious avoidance or lack of details will suggest there is more to the story and this will arouse suspicion. If you address the losses head-on, you'll leave the interviewer satisfied without having over-answered the question.

Getting a question about business losses is an opportunity to show how you turned a negative situation around or what you learned to prevent it from happening again. Here is one way to position the adverse event:

> "When we lost the Carbide account, it was a setback for our company and for our group. But we used it as a starting point to further examine our client list and uncover our vulnerable spots. I was able to provide data to the controller and sales manager that showed we were too heavily involved in this particular segment. The data sparked an initiative by the executive team to further diversify the prospects our sales team targeted. This enabled our company to halt the revenue loss it was experiencing and was the beginning of the turnaround."

SMALL OR SIGNIFICANT GAP IN EMPLOYMENT?

Acknowledge and be prepared to discuss any gap in your employment. Having a recent employment gap does not carry the stigma it once did. However, simply expecting the interviewer to understand that these are hard times will not get you far. You need to discuss your time off in a positive manner. How you handled your unexpected gap may send a signal to the employer as to how self-motivated you are and how you direct your time when not reporting to someone, regardless of your career level.

Here are tools for framing any gap you may have in your career history:

A small gap in employment (defined here as a period under six months) is not a cause for major alarm. Looking for a job is a full time job in these times. Indicate that you were engaged in your job search 35-40 hours per week for those few months; provide specifics on your activities, and outline what you learned about yourself in the process, and this should suffice for most interviewers.

If you experienced a significant gap in employment (defined here as over six months), be prepared to discuss what you did during that period in addition to your job search. Here is a sampling of my clients' activities during extended periods without full-time employment:

- Consulting work as a 1099 or through a third-party firm
- Research into franchise opportunities
- Exploration of entrepreneurial ventures
- Volunteer activities at professionally related non-profit groups
- Community service volunteer opportunities
- Personal educational and professional development initiatives
- Athletic events (advanced marathons or other elite training activities)
- World or domestic travel

- New professional internships (paid and unpaid)

Use these difficult times to position yourself as someone who faces challenges with grace and a positive attitude. Candidates who answer timidly or awkwardly may get tossed aside. Instead, prepare for the hard questions and answer them with foresight and confidence. This will help you to differentiate yourself to the prospective employer.

SPECIAL INTERVIEW SITUATIONS

Certain interview situations can challenge even the most experienced and savvy interviewee. The general rule is that when you're on any kind of interview, don't ever drop your corporate demeanor. Avoid being inappropriately casual, especially if your interviewer is extremely friendly or overly casual. Do not follow his or her lead and lose your corporate front.

This is not to say don't be friendly. But always remember there's a difference between treating the interviewer cordially and amicably, and treating the person like you've been best friends since high school. This is still an interview and the interviewer has the job at the firm—you do not.

Always keep your interview guard up. Be particularly conscious of your conduct during these situations:

- When out to lunch or dinner with the interviewer, act respectfully to all restaurant employees and to anyone you encounter on the way to or from the restaurant.
- Do not talk negatively about anyone. The interviewer may gossip, but you should never,

- ever lose sight of the fact that you are on an interview.
- Beware of situations with alcohol. Never have more than one drink, if any. Never over-indulge, even if employees of the firm do—if you over-indulge slightly, you will not be hired.

Of course, these days many interviews are conducted over the phone or via video. What do you need to know?

CHAPTER 6
HOW TO NAIL PHONE INTERVIEWS

A phone interview is an interview. Period. Make no mistake: it is not a pre-interview, an informal conversation or a brief, preliminary chat. The interview clock starts the minute you send your resume to the company or receive a call from someone who saw your LinkedIn profile, and it is certainly ticking during a phone interview.

Prepare for this type of interview the same way you would for any other interview. If you receive the call unexpectedly, step up to the role of the interviewee as best you can in the moment. You may not get another shot. Do all you can to answer the phone if it is an unplanned call. But if you are truly in a place where you cannot speak, then do let it go to voice mail and take your chances calling back.

For planned interview calls, there are special steps you can take to ensure you make the best impression:

- **Get dressed for the call as you would for the in-person interview.** If you do not want to put a full suit on, dress conservatively for the phone

interview. Even though no one will see you, you will be more on your game if you are dressed for business.
- **Ensure you have strong phone reception**, with little or no background noise.
- **Make sure your environment is quiet and serene** and will not cause distractions during your call. Eliminate visual and audible distractions.
- **Try very hard to avoid the use of a speaker phone** by either you or the interviewer.
- **Be animated and speak in as natural a manner as possible.** Display energy in your voice. In a regular interview, you have your gestures, body language, attire, and facial expressions to help convey your enthusiasm. On a phone interview, all you have is your voice to convey your spirit and enthusiasm. Focus on using your tone, pitch and words to convey your excitement about the role. I often tell clients, if it feels a little unnatural and uncomfortable for you, then you are probably doing it right.
- **Answer yes or no questions with one to three sentences.** The dialogue will be more conversational this way and more comfortable for both of you.
- **Do not multi-task while you are on the phone.** This means no reading emails, no texting, no housework, no chores, no driving, and no web browsing—unless it is to look up something said in the interview. Give your full attention to your call.

- **Smile when answering the phone.** It is said that one can "hear" a smile over the phone.
- **Take notes during the interview—even more than you would during a normal interview.** No one can see if you write a lot. Be sure to reference the notes you've taken during the interview to demonstrate solid listening skills, good recall abilities and adept application skills.

Video interviews are even more common these days, so let's make sure you nail your next video interview, too.

CHAPTER 7
SUCCESSFUL VIDEO INTERVIEWING TIPS

Employers are using video for interviewing more than ever to save time and money. No need to fly candidates in or schedule all-day interviews to capitalize on a candidate physically being in town. With an increasing global workforce where teams work remotely, video interviewing helps to see how a candidate interfaces virtually as a precursor to how they will communicate virtually with a team.

Companies typically use video for the initial screening interview. However, I have seen entire hiring processes done virtually to make a hire. How they use video during the interview process depends on the structure of the company and what the company is trying to assess.

Here are some successful video interviewing tips that can help you impress your prospective employer and allow your strengths to resonate with the hiring manager:

1. Remember, everyone thinks these types of interviews are awkward. It's not just you. Every job seeker is relatively new at interviewing via

one-way video or a video conference call, so all you have to do is to be better than your competition, who also is uncomfortable doing this type of interview. This is a new way to communicate, and it's a skill we need to acquire.

2. Practice by making a video of yourself answering sample interview questions—then watch yourself answering the questions on camera. That is what you will most likely look like on the screen to the interviewer. Make note of adjustments, mannerisms, eye contact, and background settings when applying these successful video interviewing tips.

3. Treat video interviews like a regular interview—so prepare as if it was a regular in-person interview. Do your research on the company, interviewer, job, and yourself, like you normally would for an in-person or phone interview.

4. Be yourself—on a physical interview, you would engage in small talk, have casual conversation, and allow the interviewer to get to know you as a person. Do not let the technology get in the way of this happening. People hire people they like and those with the skills—so focus on being likeable through the technology.

5. Do not lose sight of the formality of this meeting, especially if your video interview is happening at home with your webcam. Silence all pets, leave a sign on your front door to not be disturbed, and turn off phone ringers. If you have to go to an office, get there early to allow time to get settled, see how you present on their camera, and possibly do a trial run to test the equipment.

SUCCESSFUL VIDEO INTERVIEWING TIPS

6. Look at your background—is it disorganized or professional? Consider taking down some family pictures in the background and balance it out by hanging your college degree. Do you have inappropriate or awkward items within the interviewer's sight? Be sure to put forth a clean, professional image by making sure the background is free of visual distractions.

7. Fully dress for the call—yes, wear your suit pants and not your comfy Hawaiian shorts with your collared shirt and suit jacket. You may not think they will see your legs, but if you need to get up for any reason during the interview, can you say, "Awkward?"

8. Dress in solid colors. Video is not the time for that fabulous, new print tie or striped collared shirt—prints and patterns can overpower the screen and make it hard for the interviewer to watch you. It can also detract from what you're saying—and that is the whole point of the interview, yes?

9. Video interviewing can leave an impression—literally. Often employers record the interviews to compare your answers to other candidates. So be sure that what you're sharing in the interview is something you're okay with being recorded.

10. Put on your best newscaster face. On video and phone interviews, you have to be a little more animated and expressive than you would be in person to convey your enthusiasm. If you feel you are a little too happy, chances are you're probably doing it right. Test yourself by filming yourself

> answering some sample questions to see what it looks like.

Video is not the wave of the future—it is already here. We all have to embrace it and work at doing it successfully. With the successful video interviewing tips above, you are certain to have a solid chance to edge out your competition.

Is there any difference between a two-way video interview and an in-person interview?

Some say relationship building is more robust in an in-person interview, but logistics are the main difference. In a video interview, be conscious of your background and noises in your environment. Ensure your internet connection is solid and have a technical backup plan (landline, mobile, Google Voice). Remember employers often record interviews to compare answers, so make sure you're okay with everything you say being recorded. These are not necessarily causes for concern in an in-person interview.

Treat video interviews like a regular interview—prepare as if it was a regular in-person interview. Do your research on the company, interviewer, job and yourself, like you normally would for an in-person or phone interview.

Preparing for a video interview is very similar to preparing for an in-person interview.

I believe the interview, and a video interview is no different, can present opportunities on how the candidate reacts to difficulties or unexpected activities that occur. For instance, if you experience technical difficulties during the call, offer to call using a landline or cell phone. Google chat may be a viable option. I would suggest rescheduling as a last option only if trying another medium doesn't work. Seeing how a candidate reacts to adversity during the interview indicates how fluid the candidate is when things do not go as planned.

We work with our executive clients on communication delivery as well as interview research for being prepared for the interview. The main point we focus on is to prepare the candidate for various lines of questioning about themselves, how they will respond in a situation, and demonstrations of critical thinking in business scenarios.

Most candidates make the mistake of studying the company and competitors, but not themselves. Companies will ask mainly about you and your thoughts, so our successful candidates spend most of the interview prep time studying themselves and thinking through situations to respond to as practice. This premise is important, no matter what medium is used for the interview.

Remember an interview is a conversation, not an interrogation—so be prepared for them to ask you if you have any questions...

CHAPTER 8
BE ARMED FOR THE "DO YOU HAVE ANY QUESTIONS FOR US?" QUESTION

Your questions should not only come at the end of the interview when you are asked this classic question. Be prepared with questions that you can pose throughout the interview. In some interviews, the interviewer starts off by asking you for questions to determine your interest, evaluate what you already know, insert you into a stressful situation, and see how you think on your feet.

They will ask you things like:

- What do you know about us?
- What do you know about this job?
- Why do you want this job?

If this happens to you, answer the question with a sentence or two, then ask a related question that can provide you with insights for the remainder of the interview. Ask a question like one of these at the beginning of the interview, if you are allowed the opportunity:

- What issues are you hoping to address or problems are you looking to solve by hiring someone into this position?
- What interested you about my background and demonstrated that I may have what you are seeking in the next hire?

Throughout the interview, it is imperative you come across as interested and inquisitive. An interactive discussion makes things easier for you and the interviewer. So be prepared to ask for more detail or further explanations. Effective ways to do this include:

- "That certainly sounds like a different approach. Can you expand upon how the team is addressing that idea?"
- "Can you tell me more about that situation?"
- "How did the team rectify that issue?"

If you feel you must ask questions at the end of the interview, aim to have questions that reference items you discussed throughout the interview, in addition to questions that bring out new information. Some examples are:

- "What are some of the challenges the person will be experiencing within the first 90 days of this position? What about in the long-term?"
- "Who would I be interfacing with most within the first 90 days of hire?"

Ask for performance information on products and services if this information is not publicly available. If those numbers are publicly available, ask about decisions being made that can affect the future performance of those numbers.

Reference recent news about the firm in a question: "Congratulations on the firm landing a place in the Top 100 Best Places to Work listing. As outlined by the article, the firm is doing a lot of things right. In your opinion, what specifically makes people excited to work here?"

Ask for opinions and background information from the interviewer to gain understanding about the firm. "I understand you've been here a while. That is commendable. What is the company doing right to keep you here?" Or if the interviewer is a new hire, "What about the company attracted you here and made you choose to work here?"

Other questions include:

- "Of the employees who are successful within the company, what common traits would you say they exhibit?"
- "If you find that an employee does not work out, have you observed a specific reason in common as to why it was not a good match?"

In fact, if the interview is a more of a dialogue and less an inquisition, you may find you've asked all your questions during the interview and they've been satisfactorily answered. What do you then say if asked for questions at the end of this type of conversation? Use something like:

"Thank you for asking this. You thoroughly answered all of my questions throughout our discussion, making me even more excited to continue in this process of consideration. Do you have any additional questions for me?"

WHAT NOT TO ASK ON A FIRST INTERVIEW

Virtually all of the things not to ask on a first interview can be classified as being in the, "What's in it for me?" category, otherwise known as the WIIFM questions. Items that qualify for this category are questions about:

- Salary
- Time-off policies (sick days, vacation, etc.)
- Disability and FMLA policies
- Bonus and performance raises
- Employee perks and discounts
- Healthcare benefits
- Retirement plans and matches
- Education reimbursement

You want to spend the interview discussing why you're the best fit for the role. If you prove that, there will be plenty of time to discuss what the firm offers. And by waiting until they express interest, you typically gain better leverage to obtain what you want.

CHAPTER 9
HANDLING THE SALARY QUESTION

As a search firm recruiter, I would handle salary negotiations on behalf of the candidate. If you are working with a search firm recruiter, allow them to broker the terms on your behalf so you can focus your own discussions on outlining how you are the best fit for the job. But what if you are dealing with the company directly? When do you bring up the money question to ensure you are not wasting your time?

If the company is qualifying candidates correctly and asking for salary requirements, I can assure you that you are being interviewed because you meet their minimum job qualifications and you are within their budgeted salary. In these cases, you can focus on proving to the employer that you are the best person for the role.

If the company does not qualify candidates with a salary requirement question, then one of two things is most likely happening:

1. They are truly flexible in compensation, within the market standards for the position. They

might possibly pay above market rate for the best talent. You then want to demonstrate not only that you are qualified, but that you are worthy of the high-end of their compensation package.

2. The employer is unsophisticated in its recruitment practices. They may not realize that asking for salary requirements ensures that neither the candidate nor the company wastes time. Or they do this purposefully to see whether the candidate will fall in love with the job during the interview—and then accept a low-ball offer. This lack of sophistication can help you determine if this is a place where you want to work, and if you do, that you go into it fully aware of your reasons and terms.

What if you are asked about your salary needs on the interview—and on the first interview at that? If you are asked about your salary requirements at any point during the interview process, even on the first interview, answer the question. Don't avoid it or circumvent it with a passive answer. After all, you are not looking to volunteer with this company. You are looking to make a living doing something you love that enables the company to meet its goals. So don't be shy about your salary requirements, but be graceful, matter-of-fact and professional in delivering your answer.

- If asked your previous compensation, outline your total compensation number, including salary, bonuses, value of benefits, etc. Make no excuses for your salary—it is what it is.
- If asked your salary history, state your previous salaries, specifying what the bases were, plus the

HANDLING THE SALARY QUESTION

bonuses and benefits. I recommend not answering a question about base salary with a total compensation number, but state the salary with an indication of the other numbers separately.

- Don't discuss your financial situation at all. If you need the money or not is not the issue at hand. You want the recruiter/hiring manager to focus on your qualifications for the job. If the candidate was in their 20's, they would not focus on whether they were on their own or living with their parents. So as an experienced, over 40+ candidate, whether your kids are out of college and you do not need as much money as you did before, has no bearing on whether you are qualified at the market rate for that job. Don't bring it up.
- If they ask what you are looking for in your next role, realize that this is a very different question from asking what you made in past jobs. Granted, what you are looking for must be in line with your skills and what the market demands. Assuming you have those elements in line, you can answer the question in the following manner:

"I am interviewing for roles in the low 70s to high 70s salary range and I am flexible based on the nature of the responsibilities for the position."

Let's pull this apart:

- "I am interviewing for…."—this phrase is better than "I am looking for…" or "I want…" First of all, no one really cares what you are looking for or what you want. What the prospective employer wants to know is, are your expectations realistic and are you worth it? Saying "I am interviewing for…" implies that companies are calling you to interview for that role, so your intrinsic worth is implied and reinforced.
- "…in the low 70s to high 70s salary range…"—outlining a fuzzy range versus using hard numbers sends a message of flexibility in your candidacy. Most importantly, it allows you to be flexible while still enabling the employer to feel good about an offer they may present to you. If you were to give your range as "…in the 73K to 77K range…" and the company wants to offer you 72K, you have just put them in a position of thinking you might be disappointed with their offer. No employer wants to make an offer that is disappointing to their new hire. However, if you had said low 70s, an offer at 72K is well within that scope. On the flip side, if they wanted to offer you 79K, by saying high 70s, they may offer you 79K. If you state 73K to 77K, I can assure you they will most likely offer you 77K, causing you to lose 2K.
- "…and I am flexible based on the nature of the responsibilities for the position."—tacking this phrase at the end of your salary requirement will enable you to back-pedal somewhat gracefully if you misunderstood the demands of the role or you were not fully informed about its duties. If

you learn there is more responsibility involved, you can indicate that your initial salary requirement was for a less responsible role. Or, if it seems the role is not as demanding as you thought, you can indicate that you would accept a lower range for a role without senior responsibilities. It is not guaranteed that your graceful back-pedaling will win over the interviewer, but without attempting it, you almost certainly won't be considered any further.

You now have everything you need to interview confidently, but your work isn't done yet. What about after the interview?

CHAPTER 10
AFTER THE INTERVIEW

What happens after the interview?

Stay on their radar! After your first interview and any subsequent interviews, send a personal thank-you note to each person who interviewed you. It's polite to express your gratitude, and it shows you're excited about the role. Plus, you'll stand out as the person who put in the extra effort.

Here are my best tips for sending an effective thank-you note:

- Write a personal note to each person you interviewed with, and send it within 24 hours of the interview. Even if it was a group interview, where you were interviewed by several people at the same time, sending a custom note to each person is a nice touch—and an essential step in the process.
- Gather business cards from every person you speak with during the interview. This will help

- make sure you don't misspell people's names or get their titles wrong.
- Mention parts of the conversation that stood out to you in each thank-you note. This demonstrates solid listening skills and may lead to further conversation.
- Reiterate your interest in the position. If you think of something you didn't cover in the interview, this a good opportunity to provide supplemental information to reinforce your candidacy.
- Email is now an acceptable way to send a thank-you note, as long as you send it within 24 hours of the interview. It might even be a better way to send the note, due to the speed of the modern interview process.
- If you need to send a thank-you note via snail mail, I suggest you mail it by overnight mail to impress the interviewer with the strength of your interest. If other candidates are promptly emailing thank-you notes and your mailed note comes in two or three days later, you can lose out in comparison.
- Have someone read your note before sending to ensure there are no spelling or grammatical errors.

If the interviewer says they'll get back to you in a week, give it 7-10 business days for your next follow-up after your thank-you note. At that point, send an email to reiterate your interest and indicate that you're aiming to stay top of mind for the position. Tell them you know they'll get back to you as soon as they have new information, but you're just staying

AFTER THE INTERVIEW

on their radar. This approach is respectful but assertive, without making the interviewer feel harassed.

A strong follow-up is crucial to help you stand out, and to show prospective employers you're genuinely interested in working for them. It's also great networking; even if you don't land this role, you may be remembered as a thoughtful, diligent candidate if other roles come up, or if they hear of another role outside their organisation.

CONCLUSION

You now have a full range of tools, tips, and insights to help you successfully navigate the admittedly stressful interview process. If you put everything you learn here into practice, you'll have a much better than average chance of landing the job you want, and standing out to recruiters and prospective employers for all the right reasons.

Embrace your current situation and commit to applying the tools in this book. You will then position yourself to interview confidently and land a rewarding job on your terms.

On the following page, you'll find additional resources from Chameleon Resumes to help you with your resume branding, job search activities, and ongoing career development.

We wish you much success!

NEXT STEPS

Want us to personally help you to prepare for your next interview?

Hire us here: chameleonresumes.com/interview-mastery-system

Want more help from Chameleon Resumes with Job Search Consulting?

Hire us to audit your job search and fix the mistakes you may be making in your job search tactics. Invest in our Ultimate Job Search Plan here: chameleonresumes.com/ultimate-job-search

Have a question about careers and recruitment? Reach out to me here:

Lisa Rangel

lr@chameleonresumes.com

Check out the Chameleon Resumes Blog with 500+ articles on LinkedIn Profiles, interview coaching, cover letters, finding happiness at work, career transitions, and various other resume focused and job search topics. http://chameleonresumes.com/articles

ABOUT THE AUTHOR

Lisa Rangel is the founder and managing director of Chameleon Resumes, named a Forbes Top 100 Career Website. She was a moderator of LinkedIn premium groups and career blogger for 8 years. As a recruitment professional for 13 years and as a Cornell University graduate, Lisa has held management and producer roles in numerous companies, ranging from international recruitment conglomerates to focused executive search firms.

In Chameleon Resumes, she has assembled the best team of resume writers and job search consultants who all have prior search firm and corporate recruiting experience — Chameleon is the only firm of its kind! Lisa and her team know first hand which resumes get a response. They've reviewed thousands of resumes over the years and helped top recruiters and talent for top organizations, working with clients in 88 countries.

Lisa is a member of the National Resume Writers' Association and Professional Association of Resume Writers and Career Coaches. She has been featured in person, online and in print on Fast Company, Forbes, LinkedIn, Newsweek, Money, Business Insider, CNBC, BBC, Crain's New York, Chicago Tribune, CIO Magazine, American Marketing Association, eFinancial Careers, The Vault, Monster, U.S. News & World Report, Good Morning America, Fox Business News and many other reputable publications.

She is the author of nine books, creator of the Get Hired Fast job-landing training series at JobLandingAcademy.com, and a serial advice giver through her website ChameleonResumes.com. You can sign up to get advice from Lisa directly into your inbox from:

https://chameleonresumes.com/get-daily-career-tips/

linkedin.com/in/lisarangel

ALSO BY LISA RANGEL

The Job Landing Mindset

The 6-Figure Resume

Cover Letter E-Notes: The Modern Way to Land Interviews

7 Job Landing Steps to Find a Role that Makes You Happy

www.ingramcontent.com/pod-product-compliance
Lightning Source LLC
Chambersburg PA
CBHW060621080526
44585CB00013B/931